The Gang

Editor
MICHAEL BENSON

Writers
MICHAEL BENSON
PAUL W. COCKERHAM
BARRY C. ALTMARK

Photographers
BARRY C. ALTMARK
LISA M. COFFMAN
JANINE PESTEL
JOSEPH PESTEL
JAIME KOSOFSKY

Production Assistants
PAUL HALLASY
JEAN E. KREVOR
JOSE SOTO

Special thanks to Nancy Davis, Rita Eisenstein,
Norman Jacobs and Milburn Smith.

STOCK CAR SPECTACULAR

MICHAEL BENSON, EDITOR

MORE THAN
200 PHOTOS!

CRESCENT BOOKS
New York • Avenel

To Tony and Marie

Photographs copyright © 1995 Starlog Communications International
Text copyright © 1995 Random House Value Publishing, Inc.

This 1995 edition is published by Crescent Books,
distributed by Random House Value Publishing, Inc.,
40 Engelhard Avenue, Avenel, New Jersey 07001.

Random House
New York • Toronto • London • Sydney • Auckland

Printed and bound in China

A CIP catalog record for this book is available from the Library of Congress.

ISBN 0-517-12236-7

8 7 6 5 4 3 2

CONTENTS

Ricky Rudd pushes ahead!

Kyle Petty comes into the pits!

All lined up and ready to go at Charlotte.

PART I

IT'S A FAMILY BUSINESS

Stock car racing is basically a family sport. Not only for us fans, but also for the racers and teams. We'd like to introduce you to some of our favorite stock car families. First up, the Labontes . . .

LISA M. COFFMAN

When you realize that it was back in 1984 that Terry Labonte won his Winston Cup championship, it can seem surprising that this native of Corpus Christi, TX is only 37 years of age. But he was indeed the youngest driver ever to wrap up a Winston Cup championship, doing so at 27 years, 11 months of age, while driving for Billy Hagan.

Terry Labonte has had a steady 15-year career in Winston Cup racing. He has finished in the top five in points standings six times, and in the top 10 eleven times. At the start of the 1994 season, Labonte led active drivers with 444 consecutive Winston Cup starts. He could break Richard Petty's record of 513 consecutive starts in May 1996, if he keeps up the pace. He is also tied with Dale Earnhardt for career starts among active drivers, and he and Ol' Ironhead are the only drivers to have started every Winston Cup race in the 1980s and '90s.

BARRY C. ALTMARK

Terry's brother Bobby, driving the #22 Maxwell House Coffee Pontiac, was runner-up to Jeff Gordon for 1993 Winston Cup Rookie of the Year honors.

Bobby Labonte takes the high road, holding his lead on Bill Elliott.

THE WALLACES

RUSTY, KENNY & MIKE

Rusty Wallace was the 1989 Winston Cup Series Champion. He drives the #2 Miller Genuine Draft car. Up until the end of the 1993 season, Rusty drove a Pontiac. For the 1994 season, he switched to a Ford, but kept the same sponsor.

Rusty was also a car owner. He owned the #36 Cox Dry Treated Lumber Pontiac driven by his younger brother, Kenny Wallace, in the Busch Grand National (BGN) Series during the early 1990s.

Kenny has been driving on the BGN circuit since 1988. He also drove in Winston Cup races in 1991 for Kyle Petty when Petty broke his left thigh in an accident at Talladega.

In 1992, at the Phoenix International Raceway, another Wallace brother was in a Winston Cup car: Mike Wallace drove the Jimmy Means Alka Seltzer car. In fact, there were three Wallace brothers driving Winston Cup cars that year at Phoenix.

Was Rusty an absentee owner when it came to Kenny's ride? Hardly. He was hands on all the way. In fact, it seemed like he was always in the garage and pits helping out with Kenny's team. Late in the 1991 season, Kenny was unable to finish a race, so Rusty suited up and hit the track!

Kenny's #40 Dirt Devil Pontiac.

In 1991, Kenny Wallace (left) came in a close second—behind Bobby Labonte—for the Busch Grand National championship.

Kenny was named the 1989 Busch Grand National series Rookie of the Year and took the Busch Pole award at Darlington Raceway in 1990. In 1991, he came in a very close second to Bobby Labonte for the BGN championship. Kenny has the services of Crew Chief Steve "Birdie" Bird. As crew chief for the Rob Moroso BGN team, Bird helped in the championship effort.

Kenny himself knows what a winning crew chief needs to be, as he was the crew chief for Rusty's American Speed Association Silver Creek Racing series championship team. Kenny was also the crew chief for the Winston Cup series Levi Garrett team for driver Joe Ruttman.

For the Wallaces, racing is all in the family!

LISA M. COFFMAN

Left: In 1989, Kenny was voted Busch Grand National's Rookie of the Year.

Top Right: Rusty was always a hands-on owner when it comes to Kenny's ride! In 1994, Kenny began driving in the BGN series for car-owner Filbert Martocci.

Middle Right: Rusty Wallace pushes his nose ahead of Mark Martin at Bristol.

Bottom Right: Rusty is the most successful of the Wallace brothers.

LISA M. COFFMAN

77

THE BODINES

GEOFF, BRETT & TODD

The two oldest brothers, the ones who drive Winston Cup full time, drive Ford Thunderbirds, while the youngest drives a Buick in the Busch Grand National Series. Welcome to the Bodine family.

Geoff Bodine drives the #15 Motorcraft Ford, Brett Bodine drives the #26 Quaker State Ford and Todd Bodine drives the #34 Hungry Jack Buick. All three brothers, from Chemung, New York, share the same love for racing.

GEOFF

Before coming to the Winston Cup series in 1979, Geoff raced in the NASCAR Modified division, as well as in the Busch Grand National series. He started his Winston Cup career at the 1979 Daytona 500, where he even led six laps!

Geoff has won 25 Winston Cup pole positions. His lifetime earnings in Winston Cup are greater than $7 million! That places him among Winston Cup's top ten all-time money winners! He has won 14 races. His largest single purse was the $192,715 he won for taking the checkers at the Daytona 500 in 1986.

If all that wasn't enough, Geoff is not just a great driver. He is well respected on the Winston Cup circuit for his mechanical abilities as well. He introduced power steering to Winston Cup in 1981.

Geoff is also the man considered mostly responsible for the introduction of the "cool suit"—a suit designed to keep drivers cooler and therefore more alert during hot summer races.

Another innovation Geoff has helped bring about is the use of the full-face helmet. He was experimenting with them until he had a severe

Geoff Bodine's best 1993 finish was a win at the Save Mart Supermarkets 300.

LISA M. COFFMAN

*Brett Bodine's
best effort in 1993 was
a second-place finish at the
Mountain Dew Southern 500 at Darlington.
Brett finished 1.51 seconds behind Mark Martin.*

*Geoff's biggest single
paycheck was $192,715, for
winning the Daytona 500
in 1986.*

Brett qualified on the pole twice and on the front row six times in 1993.

crash at Watkins Glen. If he had been wearing an open-face helmet like most drivers did at the time, his face would not have survived the accident. His face hit the steering wheel extremely hard during the wreck, and his full-face helmet took the brunt of it, not his face. The experimenting was over at that point, and he made the switch full-time. Now most of the more experienced drivers on the Winston Cup circuit are using the full-face helmets.

After years working for Junior Johnson and Bud Moore, Geoff now owns his own car. He was in the top ten in the point standings during most of the 1993 season but bad luck during the final third of the season dropped him to 16th place in the final standings.

BRETT

Geoff's younger brother Brett Bodine drives Kenny Bernstein's #26 Quaker State Ford. Brett started his racing career in 1977 driving street stocks. He quickly moved up to the NASCAR Modified division, where he raced from 1980 to 1985.

In 1986, Brett ran his first full season of Busch Grand National races and finished second in the

Brett tries to pull away from Rusty Wallace.

14

Brett's team is owned by drag racing legend, Kenny Bernstein, and his crew chief is his brother-in-law, Donnie Richeson.

point standings for the championship, only 20 points behind champion Larry Pearson. It was the closest points battle in BGN history.

A year later Brett again ran a full BGN schedule, but added a part-time Winston Cup schedule as well. He moved to Winston Cup full time in 1988, won his first WC race in 1990 at North Wilkesboro, and has won close to $3 million!

Geoff no longer drives for the Bud Moore Motorcraft Ford team. He bought his own team for the 1994 season.

TODD

The youngest member of the clan is Todd Bodine. He is in his fourth full-time year of the BGN series. Todd also began his driving career in the NASCAR Modified Division in 1983. In 1986 he began to race in NASCAR's Late Model Stock and Grand National divisions. In June of 1991, Todd won his first BGN race. On May 22, 1993, Todd set the BGN qualifying record at Nazareth Speedway in Nazareth, Pennsylvania, clocked at 126.311 mph!

Before racing, Todd spent time crewing for

other teams in both the BGN and WC circuits. He is also a well-respected car builder, having built cars for the Nissan Factory Team (driver: Paul Newman), Chassis Dynamics, the Buck Baker Driving School and six cars for himself.

When the Bodine brothers hit the track, it's definitely a family affair!

15

THE PETTYS

LEE, RICHARD & KYLE

In 1954, 1958 and 1959, the Winston Cup championship was Lee Petty—better known as "Papa Lee" to his fans—driving ol' #42.

Then came "The King" Richard Petty, who still holds ten NASCAR records. Richard has an unbelievable 200 Winston Cup victories. It is a record that very probably will never be broken. The King started 127 Winston Cup races from the pole position—and took the checkered flag first in 61 of them. He won the Daytona 500 seven times. Fifty-five of his victories came on superspeedways. Forty-five of his wins came on short tracks.

Richard Petty won at the Martinsville Speedway in Martinsville, North Carolina 15 times alone. He won seven consecutive races at the Richmond Fairgrounds in Richmond, Virginia. He raced for 35 seasons. His first win came in 1959 on a half-mile dirt track in Columbia, South Carolina.

PETTY ENTERPRISES

The patriarch of the famous Petty racing clan, Lee Petty, now 80, was as fierce a competitor as could be found in NASCAR during the 1950s. There are legendary stories about Lee Petty's competitiveness. Once, when his son Richard wasn't cleaning his windshield fast enough during a pit stop, Lee drove out of the pits with a terrified Richard clinging to the hood. He dropped him off on the next lap. Later, when Richard started to race, his father would show him no particular mercy and bumped him off the track on more than one occasion. It is said that one time Lee put armor plating and wing nuts on the side of his Oldsmobile, so that anytime an opponent would brush too closely, his sheet metal would get shredded for his trouble.

If Bill France, Sr. can be considered the father of NASCAR, then Richard Petty has to be considered its favorite uncle. The man called "The King" has done more to popularize stock car racing than any other living being—and not solely by virtue of his racing accomplishments, which are legion. He's always been appreciative that, when all is said and done, it's the fans who pay everybody's paychecks in the sport, and he's always made sure the fans get his attention. If Richard Petty ever turned down a request for an autograph, nobody can remember when.

LISA M. COFFMAN

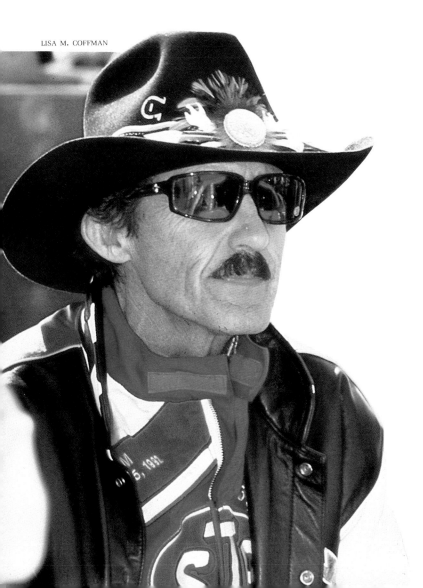

People have had a difficult time getting a handle on Kyle Petty, son of The King, Lee's grandson. His boss, car owner Felix Sabates, is no exception. "He's out there somewhere," Sabates says. "But I tell you what: if I'm racing 100 years, I hope that he will be in it 100 years with me. Kyle is not what people think he is. He is the most serene, level-headed, big-hearted blowhard. If he wasn't driving my car, I might not be in racing,"

In 14 years of Winston Cup racing, Kyle Petty has started 380 events and won seven of them. He's pulled down $5,619,049 in prize money, including the largest single purse ever awarded— $294,450 for the 1990 Goodwrench 500.

Critics cite Kyle's occasional foray into country music as indicative of his not having the focus or drive to be a true champion like his father, yet he is unfazed by the comparison. "When I first stepped into a race car, I didn't have any expectations for where my career would go. Growing up as I did as a Petty, I knew that you could have some really good years and some bad ones as well."

77

"I think the biggest problem we had in 1993 [a year he finished fifth in the points] was that the driver and the car were out of sync," Kyle says. "Every time the car ran really well, I drove really bad. Felix says the hair got in my eyes. When I felt that I could drive, the car just wouldn't work with me. I took us out of contention several times. Hey, I'll be the first to admit to brain fade."

BARRY C. ALTMARK

In 1992, Richard's last year as an active driver, he was asked why he was retiring.

"Age has something to do with it," the 54-year-old King said. "And not winning any races since 1984 also has something to do with it."

What are King Richard's four most memorable moments? No problem. He has made a list:

1. Starting in his 1,000th race in 1986 at the Michigan International Speedway on Father's Day where his three daughters gave the official order to start the engines.

2. Winning his 200th race at the Daytona Firecracker 400 in 1984 with President Reagan watching in the stands.

3. Clinching his seventh Winston Cup championship at Ontario Motor Speedway in 1979.

4. Winning his first championship in 1964.

In the two years since his retirement from active racing he has remained on the scene as the owner of the STP team, sponsor of his old ride.

The greatest tribute to Richard as a driver and as a man is the respect shown to him by his fans and colleagues both on and off the track. He always

The 1993 season was Richard's first year out of the cockpit, and he felt the absence. His race team has struggled, thanks to the many demands on The King's time. "It's true," says the head honcho of the STP racing team. "I knew a year ago that I'd be missing not driving a race car anymore, but I didn't know just how much. It took awhile to get over that feeling, and maybe my thinking got clouded along the way. This year [1994], I'm a bunch more relaxed. I still miss driving, probably always will. But we're fixing to get ol' No. 43 back to winning again."

Kyle's ahead by a nose!

Kyle goes high as Geoff Bodine tries to pass on the inside.

Kyle finished fourth at Talladega in 1993, and 13th in 1994.

finds time to greet his fans and help out with a worthy cause.

Now Kyle Petty has taken over Grandpapa Lee's #42 and has proven again and again that he is a driver to contend with. Kyle has been racing Winston Cup races since 1980, but he didn't get serious about it until 1989.

He was torn between careers, you see. He's an accomplished country and western singer as well as one of the superstars of the stock car track. He toured, opening for Randy Travis.

But in 1989 Kyle joined the Felix Sabates racing team, stopped performing and devoted himself full time to Winston Cup racing. In 1990, Kyle took the pole at the Goodwrench 500 at the North Carolina Motor Speedway. He then went on to

One of King Richard's old cars currently resides in the Motorsports Hall of Fame.

In the garage, Kyle looks for just the right tool.

Kyle started on the pole for the 1993 Daytona 500 but finished 31st in the race when he was swept into a wreck.

Here's a view that lots of drivers got of King Richard's car!

Richard Petty's last race took place at the Atlanta Motor Speedway in 1992. He didn't finish however, as ol' #43 caught on fire!

Kyle drives the Mello Yello Pontiac for team owner Felix Sabates.

Mello Yello has extended its sponsorship of this team to the year 2000.

win the race and took home a check for $294,000. Sabates was so pleased with Kyle's Goodwrench 500 victory that he bought his driver a Rolls Royce!

Unfortunately, 1991 was not such a great year for Kyle. He was sidelined for a big part of the season, twelve races, because of a broken thigh suffered in a crash at the Winston 500 at Talladega.

In 1992, Kyle got a new crew chief, Robin Pemberton, who started his career working for, you guessed it, Richard Petty.

DARRELL & MICHAEL

Here's a brother combo that has become a NASCAR fixture. The older brother owns and races his own Winston Cup team and has won the Winston Cup championship three times. He is Darrell Waltrip, driver of the #17 Western Auto Chevrolet Lumina.

The younger brother, driving the #30 Pennzoil Pontiac, is Michael Waltrip. Back in 1983, Michael was the National Champion in the Charlotte-Daytona Dash Series. He was voted the Most Popular Driver in that Dash Series in 1983 and 1984.

Michael is now in his ninth full-time season in the Winston Cup series. His cars are owned and prepared by car-owner, Chuck Rider, and his new crew chief, Doug Hewitt. He's also a regular on the Busch Grand National series. Whenever the two series compete together—the Busch Grand National race on Saturday and the Winston Cup race on Sunday—you'll see Michael in both races. He seems to have better luck in his Busch Grand National car. He has seven wins to his credit in this series. While his best Winston Cup finish was sec-

BARRY C. ALTMARK

Michael Waltrip drives the #30 Pennzoil Pontiac.

In 1983, Michael was the Charlotte-Daytona Dash Series Champion.

BARRY C. ALTMARK

Michael is in his ninth full season as a Winston Cup driver.

Darrell won the Winston Cup championship in 1981, 1982 and 1985. He has won 84 Winston Cup races so far in his career.

ond at the 1988 Miller High Life 500 in Pocono. Michael won "The Winston Open" in 1991 and 1992 at Charlotte Motor Speedway. Unfortunately these are not point races so he still hasn't won his first Winston Cup race, but he has 29 top-ten finishes in the last four years. He has won more than $2.5 million in Winston Cup races.

This 6'5" native of Owensboro, Kentucky took on a new challenge last year: He got married. After a strong second half last year, Michael looks forward to the 1994 season.

"What we did on the track last fall was important for all of us, but what is more important is

Michael Waltrip moves ahead of Ernie Irvan in a Busch Grand National race.

23

Some still consider Darrell the "original bad boy of NASCAR." He has never been afraid to speak up about what he believes in, even if he happens to be talking to NASCAR officials at the time.

BARRY C. ALTMARK

LISA M. COFFMAN

Michael has the dubious honor of being involved in the worst crash in racing history that someone walked away from. On April 7, 1990 at Bristol Raceway he was involved in a wreck that completely demolished his car.

PENNZOIL RACING

what everyone had done at the shop all winter long to get ready for this season. I'm more excited about the prospects for 1994 than I am about what we accomplished late in 1993," says Michael.

Big brother Darrell won the Winston Cup championship in 1981, 1982 and 1985. He has won 84 Winston Cup races so far in his career. In 1972 he started his winning ways by taking the USAC stock car race in Nashville, TN.

Darrell won the Olsonite Driver of the Year

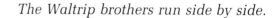

The Waltrip brothers run side by side.

PENNZOIL RACING

*"I'm excited about the prospects for 1994,"
says Michael.*

Award in 1979, 1981 and 1982; the National Motorsports Press Association Driver of the Year Award in 1977, 1981 and 1982; and the Auto Racing Digest Driver of the Year Award in 1981 and 1982.

The eldest racing Waltrip was named the NASCAR Winston Cup Most Popular Driver in 1989 and 1990. He has won three International Race of Champions races and holds the modern record for most Winston Cup victories in two consecutive seasons (1981–82) with 24. Darrell also became the first driver to win $6 million in his career in 1985, the first to win $7 million (1986), $8 million (1988), $9 million (1989) and $10 million (1990).

Some still consider Darrell the "original bad boy of NASCAR." He has never been afraid to speak up about what he believes in, even if he happens to be talking to NASCAR officials at the time. Darrell says, "I wanted to have an impact on the sport and be able to change the things that are wrong with it. I want people to respect and appreciate me for what I am, and to know that all I ever wanted was to win races."

Michael has the dubious honor of being involved in the worst crash in racing history that someone walked away from. On April 7, 1990 at Bristol Raceway he was involved in a wreck that completely demolished his car. The crash took place on lap 171 when Michael and Robert Pressley collided in the second turn. His car shot up the track, smashed into the crossover gate, and then the car's right side slammed into the end of the concrete wall. With the tremendous impact, his car disintegrated around him. Kenny Wallace, coming around the turn, missed Michael by about an inch. Michael managed to walk—well, limp—away from the crash which, if nothing else, proves the effectiveness of NASCAR's strict safety requirements.

Both Darrell and Michael have the drive and determination to win. Look for both brothers to visit Victory Lane many more times.

A little service for the Pennzoil Pontiac!

PART II

SAYING GOODBYE

Stock car racing, in terms of danger, doesn't compare with other sports—and fans, rightfully so, worry about their racing heroes in a way unfamiliar to fans of athletes who compete in other arenas. We do not generally worry about a basketball player losing his life during a game, but every time the cry goes out for the gentlemen to start their engines, race car drivers put their lives on the line. And so, when tragedy occurs, there is a temptation for some to say, "He knew the risks." True enough. But that doesn't make saying goodbye any easier.

LISA M. COFFMAN

BARRY C. ALTMARK

As we'll always remember Alan Kulwicki—behind the wheel of a race car.

Davey gave it quite a run for the 1992 Winston Cup championship. He was running strong in the 1993 season and many people thought that it was Davey's year. Davey will be remembered as a dedicated father, husband, racer and sportsman.

ALAN KULWICKI

NASCAR FAMILY BIDS FAREWELL

On April 1, 1993, en route to the Food City 500 Winston Cup race, the racing world lost Alan Kulwicki. Alan, and three others aboard, died when their plane crashed on approach near Bristol, Tennessee. Alan was the reigning NASCAR Winston Cup Champion.

Alan's theme song during his career—and especially during his championship season—was Frank Sinatra's "(I Did It) My Way." He had offers to join big-money teams, but wanted to achieve his racing goals on his own. Sometimes he would race with no sponsors and only one car (no backups). He had a Mighty Mouse patch sewn to his uniform sleeve. He even called his team the "Underbirds." They were always chasing after teams better financed and sponsored. Then, the Kulwicki team secured the Hooters sponsorship, and 1992 looked great. Alan started in 29 races, won twice, took two pole positions and won the championship by the

Soon after Alan won the 1992 Winston Cup championship, no less an authority than Richard Petty put Kulwicki's accomplishment in perspective: "It's almost impossible to win the title as a driver/owner, but he's done it," Petty said. "He overcame the odds with determination, skill and luck."

Alan is survived only by his father, who now owns the racing team.

Kulwicki at the start of the 1992 Winston 500 at Talladega Superspeedway.

Alan always found time for his fans.

BARRY C. ALTMARK

second narrowest margin in NASCAR history. (Only Richard Petty won by less.)

It was quite a blow to the NASCAR family to hear of his death. More than 1,000 people came to his memorial service in Charlotte, North Carolina. In recognition of Alan's notorious Polish victory lap, Michael Waltrip and Rusty Wallace both celebrated their wins at Bristol that weekend with Polish victory laps. What's a Polish victory lap? When Alan won the championship at Atlanta Motor Speedway last November, instead of taking the customary victory lap, he turned his car around and went in the opposite direction (clockwise) around the track. When Michael Waltrip won the Busch Grand National race he also dedicated the win to Alan. Rusty Wallace vowed to repeat a Polish victory lap each time he won a race that year. He kept his promise for all three of his wins. After Rusty's win of the Food City 500, Dale Earnhardt who came in a very close second said, "I congratulate Rusty and hope everybody will say a prayer for Alan and his family."

Alan is survived only by his father, who now owns the racing team. The elder Kulwicki has asked Felix Sabates to run the team and find a buyer for it, keeping the team intact if at all possible. Sabates is the owner of Kyle Petty's Mello

Yello Pontiac and Bobby Labonte's Maxwell Coffee Thunderbird. He asked Jimmy Hensley to drive the Kulwicki cars at North Wilkesboro, Martinsville and Talladega. Hooters pulled its sponsorship and Bojangles sponsored the team for those three races.

Strangely, in a 1992 interview, Alan stated that if anything should happen to him, he would like Jimmy Hensley to take over the driving duties for him.

Kulwicki leads the field down the front straightaway in his orange Dodge Daytona during the 1992 Darlington edition of the International Race of Champions.

An efficient pit stop for Kulwicki's #7 Hooters Ford!

LISA M. COFFMAN

BARRY C. ALTMARK

and keep it together. It would be a shame to dismantle this championship caliber team.

The team was eventually sold to driver Geoff Bodine, who now runs the team as a driver/owner.

"I'm honored," says Hensley, "Alan and I would speak at different tracks. We never stood around and talked. I think one reason is that Alan liked my style. I don't tear up a lot of stuff. Alan came up that way."

What was the future for Kulwicki racing? Sabates had four serious buyers who would buy the team

Dale Earnhardt was asked by the IROC officials to fill in for Alan at the Talladega race. Dale donated all his winnings to Alan's favorite charities and kept the points earned in Kulwicki's name. The racing family always remembers one of their own.

—BARRY C. ALTMARK

BARRY C. ALTMARK

SO LONG, DAVEY

WITH LOVE & COURAGE, THE ALLISONS PUSH AHEAD

The past couple of years will hold wonderful and dreadful memories for Bobby Allison. In 1993 Bobby was nominated and inducted to International Motorsports Hall of Fame. His race team was coming together nicely and was getting stronger. But, 1993 also saw the death of his eldest son and rising Winston Cup star, Davey. 1992 saw the death of his younger son, Clifford Allison.

Davey died in a helicopter crash on his way to the Talladega Superspeedway to watch Neil Bon-

BARRY C. ALTMARK

The #28 Havoline Ford of Davey Allison.

Davey gets ready to start the Darlington edition of the International Race of Champions— a race he won!

30

LISA M. COFFMAN

With Davey gone, this car is now being driven by Ernie Irvan.

Davey straps himself in!

Davey in victory lane at Darlington with his lovely family.

Bobby Allison, right, a legendary stock car driver in his own right, was the owner of the Jimmy Spencer driven Raybestos car in 1993.

Davey Allison was a winner in every sense of the word.

nett practice for his return to Winston Cup racing at the Die Hard 500. Davey was one of the brightest stars on the Winston Cup series. He started racing in the Limited Sportsman division at Birmingham International Speedway in Alabama in 1979. In 1981 he moved up to the NASCAR Grand American series and also raced in the ARCA series. In 1983 he raced in the Busch Grand National series, All Pro, ASA and Grand American series. He was named the ARCA Rookie of the Year in 1984. In 1985 he entered his first Winston Cup race at Tal-

ladega, finishing tenth. In 1987 Davey drove for the Ranier-Lundy Winston Cup team. In 1988, crew chief and engine builder Robert Yates bought the team, and the partnership of Davey Allison, Robert Yates and Larry McReynolds was founded. Each year this team got stronger and stronger. Davey gave it quite a run for the 1992 Winston Cup championship. He was running strong in the 1993 season and many people thought it was going to be Davey's year.

Davey will be remembered as a dedicated father,

The Havoline crew goes to work.

LISA M. COFFMAN

husband, racer and sportsman. From grade school on, Davey always knew what he wanted to do with his life—race.

Bobby's youngest son, Clifford died from his crash while practicing for the Busch Grand National Detroit Gasket 200 at Michigan, in August 1992. Clifford was a regular in the ARCA Super Car series and was beginning a promising career in the Busch Grand National series.

Besides these awful tragedies Bobby has many highlights to note. Bobby is the 1983 Winston Cup Champion and six-time NASCAR Most Popular Driver (1971, 1972, 1973, 1981, 1982 and 1983). Some more of his credits: 86 Winston Cup victories, 57 Winston Cup pole positions, winner of the 1980 IROC series, competed in six Indy Car races and won

Davey: In a thoughtful mood.

Davey Allison after one of his 19 Winston Cup victories.

more than $7 million as a driver. He also holds titles for Modified and Late Model Sportsman series. After retiring from driving, from 1988 to 1993, Bobby owned and ran the #12 Meineke Ford Winston Cup team. He also owns and operates Allison Race Cars with his brother Donnie Allison in Hueytown, Alabama. They manufacture and prepare stock cars and have recently started a new national craze, Legend Cars.

The last few years may not hold the best memories for the Allison family, but—with love and courage—together this family will push ahead.

—BARRY C. ALTMARK

Davey winning in a Dodge? Well, in the IROC series, all drivers ride identical cars.

35

NEIL BONNETT DIES AT DAYTONA

HE WAS 47

You have to wonder just how many hits The Alabama Gang can take.

After losing brothers Cliff (1992) and Davey (1993) Allison, The Gang saw Neil Bonnett die February 11, 1994 after his Chevrolet Lumina slid in Daytona International Speedway's Turn 4 during practice for the Daytona 500, hitting the outside wall head-on. Popular throughout NASCAR—both as a competitor and as a color commentator for CBS, TBS and TNN—the native of Hueytown, Alabama was 47.

What typified Bonnett more than anything else was the man's dogged determination to come back from adversity. Winston Cup fans fully appreciated the sad irony that his death came in the midst of another comeback.

Racing for the Wood Brothers in 1989, Bonnett achieved nine top-10 finishes before suffering a broken sternum during the September race at Dover. He sat out the next three events, but came back with two more top 10s during the final three races of the year.

There was talk of his retiring—his Winston Cup career went back 15 years at that point—but he was determined to come back strong in 1990. Yet at Darlington that year, in only the fifth race of the season, Bonnett's No. 21 Citgo Ford Thunderbird was involved in a multi-car wreck on the main straight that left him with serious head injuries, and what developed into a recurring case of memory loss.

Doctors advised Bonnett to hang up his helmet, but it wasn't long before television chose to reap the benefits of Bonnett's easy-going nature. He became a popular and knowledgeable racing analyst, and a familiar sight in the garage area on race day, with his navy blazer and headphones.

But being out of the driver's seat ate away at the soul of a man who had won 18 Winston Cup events in the course of his career—as well as nearly $4 million in prize money. He kept involved by helping out his son, David, launch a Busch Grand National career, but it wasn't really enough for Bonnett.

Nobody knew this better than Bonnett's fishing and hunting buddy, Dale Earnhardt. Last May, Earnhardt offered Bonnett a chance to do some testing for Richard Childress Racing. The six-time Winston Cup champion was looking for advice from Bonnett, while at the same time offering him a no-pressure scenario to get some seat time. A week later, Bonnett received medical clearance to race again.

"You can't walk away from a sport you've spent your entire life around," Bonnett said last year in an interview. "Television was a good avenue for me to get involved in racing again. It opened the

LISA M. COFFMAN

Why did Neil come out of retirement? Well, being out of the driver's seat ate away at the soul of a man who had won 18 Winston Cup events in the course of his career—as well as nearly $4 million in prize money. He kept involved by helping out his son, David, launch a Busch Grand National career, but it wasn't really enough for Bonnett.

door to come back and be around all my friends. But it also stirred up that interest to get back inside of a race car."

Bonnett was back up to speed in no time at all, and RCR entered a second car for Bonnett for the July race at Talladega, a few miles from Bonnett's home.

But what had been planned as a reunion for The Alabama Gang turned to tragedy with the July 12 helicopter crash that took Davey Allison's life the following day. Allison and Red Farmer (who survived with minor injuries) flew to the track to watch David Bonnett test a car. It was Neil Bonnett who first arrived on the scene and pulled the pair from the wreckage.

The race itself was almost anticlimactic at that point, in spite of a tumbling wreck into the fence in the early going, but Bonnett was elated to be back, in spite of everything.

"I ran the full range of emotions that week," Bonnett recalled last November. "What happened to the Allison family was a tragedy. That was weighing on my mind, but when I qualified it was a ton of weight off my shoulders. I was told to quit and I made it back. Now the decision to race was mine and that put me more at ease."

BARRY C. ALTMARK

JAIME KOSOFSKY

Neil is survived by his wife Susan, son David, and a daughter, Christen.

Country Time powdered drink mix saw a great opportunity in sponsoring the congenial and widely recognized Bonnett, and last fall set up, with Phoenix Racing, a limited six-race schedule for 1994, with Neil piloting the striking pink-and-yellow #51.

The Daytona 500 was to be the new team's first race. Strong winds were blowing off the beach that Friday morning. Bonnett was turning in practice laps at around 170 mph shortly after noon when the Lumina slid in the high-banked fourth turn. It headed down to the track apron, and then up the banking before hitting the outside wall nearly head-on.

Rescue workers at the scene reported that the force of impact apparently caused enough structural weakening within the car to allow Bonnett's head to strike the wall. He was pronounced dead at Halifax Medical Center in Daytona Beach at 1:17 P.M., but official word was withheld for a few hours. Bonnett's wife Susan was driving to Daytona that afternoon, and NASCAR president Bill France Jr. had state troopers in Georgia and Florida seeking her out. She learned of the death when she arrived at the track at 5:00 P.M.

Bonnett was laid to rest in ceremonies in Hueytown the following Monday, Valentine's Day. He is survived by his wife Susan, son David, and a daughter, Christen.

—PAUL W. COCKERHAM

Bonnett was turning in practice laps at around 170 mph shortly after noon when the Lumina slid in the high-banked fourth turn. It headed down to the track apron, and then up the banking before hitting the outside wall nearly head-on.

PART III

SUPERSTARS

Handsome Harry Gant, driver of the No. 33 Skoal Bandit Chevrolet Lumina owned by Leo Jackson, is hanging up his helmet this season after more than 20 years behind the wheel, a career where he won 18 races and nearly $8 million.

In March of 1986 he won his first superspeedway race (Motorcraft 500) at Atlanta. In March of 1993 he won his third super-speedway race at the same place—Atlanta. This driver is Morgan Shepherd and he is in his third year of driving the #21 Citgo Ford Thunderbird.

BARRY C. ALTMARK

BARRY C. ALTMARK

Now that he has started to master what some had considered an overly aggressive driving style, Ernie Irvan has developed into one of the superstars of Winston Cup Racing. Now driving the No. 28 Robert Yates Texaco/Havoline Ford Thunderbird made famous by the late Davey Allison, Irvan has to be considered one of the favorites to win the 1995 Winston Cup championship.

Some people believe that Jeff Gordon may be the most gifted driver ever to wrap his hands around a steering wheel. They have a case, if his meteoric career to date is any indication. Gordon, all of 22 years of age, is in his third season in NASCAR, his second in Winston Cup. He is a product of the U.S. Auto Club's open-wheel divisions, and it seems as though it was only yesterday that he was winning every time you turned on "Saturday Night Thunder."

39

RUSTY WALLACE

The #2 Miller Genuine Draft Ford Thunderbird is piloted by Rusty Wallace. 1993 saw many wonderful things for this team and especially Rusty. When the Winston Cup series went to Atlanta for the final race of the year, the championship was still a real possibility for Rusty. In early October his crew, under the new direction of Buddy Parrott, not only won the Unocal Pit Crew Championship at Rockingham but set a new record time of 22.454 seconds.

Alas, it wasn't to happen last year. Even though Rusty won the Hooters 500, he took a close second in last year's championship. Let's take a closer look at Rusty's career.

Even though Rusty won the Hooters 500 in Atlanta in 1993, he still finished second to Dale Earnhardt in the WC point standings.

In 1993, Rusty had a chance to win the Winston Cup championship right up until the final race.

Rusty started his career in 1973, driving for the Central Auto Racing Association (CARA), where he was presented the Rookie of the Year Award.

Between 1974–78, Rusty won more than 200 races for the CARA.

In 1979, Rusty moved to USAC— and again won the Rookie of the Year Award.

RUSTY THE ROOKIE

Rusty started his career in 1973 and won the Rookie of the Year award in the Central Auto Racing Association that same year. There he won more than 200 features from 1974–1978 when he joined the USAC series in 1979. There again he took the Rookie of the Year award in 1979. He started racing on the ASA series and won their championship in 1983. While still racing the ASA series he tried his hand in Winston Cup. In 1984 he was voted Rookie of the Race at the Southern 500 at Darlington and Winston Cup Rookie of the Year. He won his first Winston Cup race in 1986 (Valleydale 500 at Bristol). His first pole came at the Michigan International Speedway in 1987 (Miller High Life 400). In 1989 he won "The Winston" at Charlotte and of course that same year he won his Winston Cup championship.

Wallace won the ASA championship in 1983.

41

In 1984, Rusty won his third Rookie award, this time in Winston Cup!

This is the #2 Miller Genuine Draft Pontiac. In 1994, Rusty has kept the same number and the same sponsor— but he's now driving a T-Bird.

Rusty earned his first Winston Cup pole position in 1987 at the Southern 500 at Darlington.

Rusty won his first Winston Cup race in 1986. It was the Valleydale 500 at Bristol.

Rusty comes in for gas at the First Union 400.

PENSKE & PARROTT

In 1991, Rusty joined with Roger Penske and set out for another Winston Cup championship. That year saw a great deal of ups and downs. This brand new team finished tenth in the Winston Cup points with two wins and two pole positions. In the middle of 1992 it was decided that a new crew chief was needed. The team needed something more, what they got was Buddy Parrott. Buddy is a seasoned veteran who has helped Darrell Waltrip, Morgan Shepherd, Joe Ruttman, Derrike Cope, Ricky Craven and Richard Petty into victory lane.

The biggest and boldest change for this team going into the 1994 season is the changing of manufacturers. There are now Fords instead of Pontiacs in the #2 garage.

On any given weekend, Rusty can be first under the checkered flags.

43

"Don't be all balls and no brains!"

RUSTY'S RIOT ACT

WALLACE SPEAKS UP AT PRE-DAYTONA 500
DRIVER MEETING

The usually festive Speedweek 1994 at the Daytona International Speedway, the prelude to stock-car racing's premiere event, the Daytona 500, had taken a tragic turn—and then, when attempts to "return to normal" had finally kicked into gear, tragedy returned for an encore.

That was the way it was when Neil Bonnett, the beloved veteran driver who was attempting a limited comeback on the Winston Cup circuit, was killed in a one-car accident during practice on February 11, 1994.

Three days later, the day of Bonnett's funeral, rookie Rodney Orr was also killed in practice, also a one-car accident. Many drivers sunk into a grim silence over the loss, and yes, although they won't admit it, the fear.

But not Rusty Wallace. Wallace took it upon himself to deliver the verbal warning, pep talk and refresher course.

"I was responding to a problem that's been ongoing, but after the two deaths, that was a little extra that shoved me over the side," Wallace told a reporter on February 18, the Friday before the 500.

At a drivers' meeting the previous day, Wallace—without pointing fingers—read the riot act regarding driver etiqutte, and etiquette that is in place not because this is a sport for gentlemen but because it is what allows three-abreast racing on banked turns (the sport's bread & butter, afterall) without a slaughter taking place.

Rusty Wallace had a few angry words for his colleagues before the 1994 Daytona 500.

44

"I think a lot of it had to do with a lack of caution," Wallace said. "I think a lot of drivers have gotten way too aggressive."

Did the message stick? "You can't fix them [the drivers] all. There are some people, it'll go right over their heads."

Not that he was blaming anyone for the fatalities. Wallace's theory on the deaths was: "There were problems there that I believe came from some of the setups the teams were using." He was referring to the softer coil springs some teams were using to lower the car and make it more efficient against the wind. The springs, Wallace claimed, were making the cars unstable when hitting bumps on the track.

BARRY C. ALTMARK

Wallace said, "I think a lot of drivers have gotten way too aggressive."

Rusty's Riot Act worked. The 1994 Daytona 500 was run safely.

"I was responding to a problem that's been ongoing, but after the two deaths, that was a little extra that shoved me over the side," Wallace said.

45

THE OVER THE WALL GANG!

WALLACE'S RED-HOT PIT CREW
STRIKES FEAR INTO THE COMPETITION!

by Paul W. Cockerham

MOORESVILLE, N.C.—These days, to work on a top-flight NASCAR pit crew, it's not enough to be simply a great mechanic. You have to be in great shape, too.

Just ask the Over-The-Wall Gang.

The Gang—Penske South's Miller Genuine Draft pit crew—has been putting a real scare into the competition on the Winston Cup circuit so far this season. It seems that nearly every time driver Rusty Wallace pits for service during caution periods, he gains two or three positions simply because the Gang works faster than anybody else on pit row.

Wallace credits a new crew chief—and the physical conditioning program he helped develop—for much of the team's recent success.

"Before Buddy Parrott joined us a crew chief last year, we were a bit unfocused and disorganized," says Wallace, who owns the team along with Roger Penske and Don Miller. "But he has turned our crew into a crack unit."

Parrott has a reputation for being somewhat restless, putting in relatively short stints with some of the best shops on the circuit before retiring briefly during the '80s. But the lure of stock cars proved too great to resist; Parrott "unretired" and was crew chief at Radius Motor Sport for Ted Musgrave when Wallace called him late last season. Parrott figures he's finally found a home with Penske.

"There's no doubt about the level of commitment that this operation has toward winning," Parrott said. "It's the pinnacle of my career to be involved with an operation as good as Penske. I had to pinch myself the first month I was here. The operation is first class, everything a crew chief could want."

Parrott has added some key personnel to the pit crew, whose members now include Scott Robinson as the jack man ("the best in the busi-

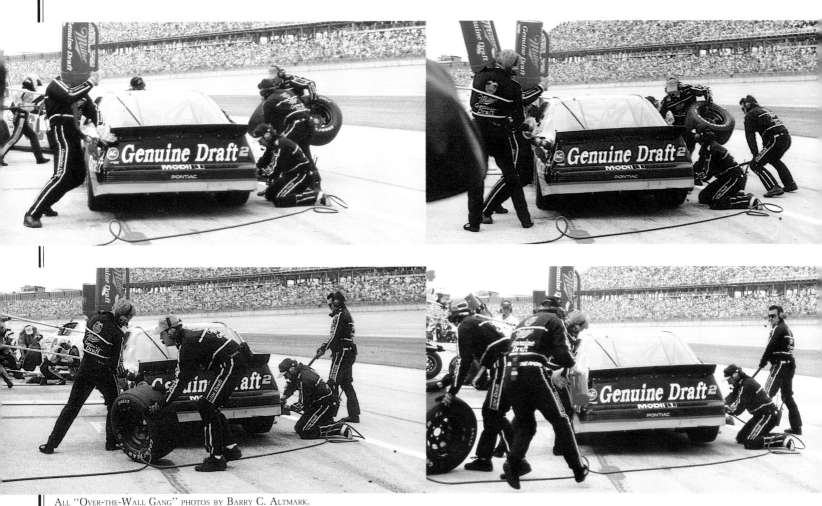

ness," says Parrott.); Bill Wilburn, front-tire changer; Brad Parrott (a son), rear tire changer; Scott Cluka and Todd Parrott ("my oldest"), tire carriers; Earl Barban and Nick Ollila, gas men; Rocky Owenby, catch-can man; among others.

He has also made some changes in pit-stop strategy, but it's his physical fitness program, conducted at Penske South's shops here, that is unique among NASCAR teams.

"I first made calisthenics a part of training back when I was with Darrell Waltrip. But that's not what we do here," Parrott says. "Everything is high tech. I told Rusty what I wanted to do, and he pretty much gave me a blank check to shape these guys up."

The facility has a complete fitness room, with exercise bikes, treadmills, stair-climbing machines, weight machines, and free weights. Aerobics classes are held regularly. The progress of team members, who are required to work out for an hour at least three times a week, is regularly monitored by a physical trainer.

"The guys call him Jack LaLanne, but his real name is Bob Pressley," says Parrott. "He comes from Carolina Medical Center, and he sure does keep us moving—although he's not beyond playing head games with the boys.

"Today he's supposed to bring in an aerobics instructor who is drop-dead beautiful—*that* should get 'em pumped up! You keep a guy looking forward to coming to work," he says.

"Physical conditioning is important," Parrott adds. "Not only do you need strength to lift tires and fuel cans, but you need agility to jump over the pit wall when the car comes in, great manual dexterity, and superb eye-hand coordination."

The program has helped the crew gel as a unit as well.

"The guys really look forward to it—it gives them a break from all the hard work they put into the cars," Parrott says, "and working out in the room together as a team."

Indeed. The Gang has such a strong identity that NASCAR souvenir stands now do a brisk business selling Over-The-Wall Gang T-shirts.

The crew's performance has helped Wallace finish in the top five nearly every time out the last two seasons, a record that included many visits to Victory Lane. And at the 1993 season-opening Daytona 500, their skill was helping Wallace, who started 34th, to a certain top-five finish before a spectacular accident knocked the Miller Genuine Draft Pontiac out of the running.

"All the hard work is done at the shop during the week," Parrott says. "On Sundays, we're out there to show off and have fun."

Give the Rusty Wallace team 16 seconds and they'll change four tires, put two cans of gas in the tank, and get him out of the pits in time to advance two more positions.

47

DALE EARNHARDT

THE INTIMIDATOR!

It is said that Dale Earnhardt's take-no-prisoners driving style closely resembles that of his late father Ralph Earnhardt, a noted NASCAR dirt track warrior from the '50s who won the sportsman title in 1956. An interesting style it is, too.

Dale Earnhardt has never been the best of qualifiers throughout his career, which is now in its 20th Winston Cup season. The black No. 3 GM Goodwrench Chevy Lumina will often start towards the middle or the back of the pack, but it isn't usually long before "Ol' Ironhead" (another nickname Dale's fellow drivers have hung on him) starts charging through the field.

Betting that the man they call The Intimidator will nail down a record-tying seventh Winston Cup crown in 1994 is about as close to a sure thing as you'll find in stock car racing.

BARRY C. ALTMARK

Dale's talent has made him the wealthiest driver in American motorsports history, with total winnings, as of the end of the '93 season, of $20.8 million, of which more than $19.5 million has come from Winston Cup competition (the balance comes from his success in the International Race of Champions series, which he won in 1990).

He won the Winston Cup title in 1980, 1986, 1987, 1990, 1991 and 1993, and as of the start of the 1994 season had 59 career wins in 449 starts—sixth on the all-time list.

According to the official scorers, the car leading at the start-finish line led the whole lap!

Dale made his first WC start at the 1975 World 600 in Charlotte.

Car-owner Richard Childress says, "I knew the first time I saw him drive I wouldn't mind having him drive my car."

In Victory Lane, Dale gets a kiss from daughter Taylor Nicole.

The black #3 Goodwrench
Chevy Lumina of Dale
Earnhardt!

Because Earnhardt is not the
best of qualifiers, he often
has to start races from the
middle of the pack.

BARRY C. ALTMARK

Dale's crew gets ready for
a pitstop.

"You establish your territory," Ralph Earnhardt used to tell Dale, which he does, in spades. He is also so talented at overtaking cars that the mere sight of Dale coming up in a driver's rear-view mirror, with that driver knowing he has to cope with Dale's arsenal of short-track moves, is often enough to send that car skidding out of control.

Confidence is a big part of the Dale Earnhardt story. His faith in his own driving ability is such that he can quickly figure out the limits of a car's performance, and his touch is so deft that he can take a car beyond those limits for extended periods, when he needs to.

His first Winston Cup start came in the 1975 World 600 at Charlotte. He started 33rd, and finished 22nd. Apparently the guy finishing right behind him was the most impressed. That man was Richard Childress, who today is the owner of the

Dale waits for the magic words: "Gentlemen, start your engines."

Earnhardt's Chevy is pushed into place on the starting grid.

The most famous helmet in American motorsports.

A familiar picture: Dale in Victory Lane.

Earnhardt moves past Mark Martin on the outside.

GM Goodwrench Racing Team and Earnhardt's boss.

"I knew the first time I saw him drive I wouldn't mind having him drive my car," Childress says. "But I had never considered being just a car owner at that point. When I finally made that decision back in 1981, it was the toughest decision I had ever made. Looking back, of course, it was also the smartest."

"We're going full bore for number seven," says Earnhardt. "There will never be another Richard Petty, but seven—and then eight—championships are goals of mine, because I would be part of a record, too."

54

Ever wonder why they call him "The Intimidator"?

Dale Earnhardt: Re-writing the record books!

A crew member in the garage makes sure everything is perfect.

Ready to go at Rockingham!

BILL ELLIOTT

THE MOST POPULAR MAN IN AMERICAN MOTOR SPORTS!

Songs have been written about him . . . and when it comes to vote for the fans' most popular driver in the Winston Cup series the other drivers don't even bother to wait for the results. Everyone goes over to Bill Elliott and congratulates him.

Elliott has a conference with his crew in the garage.

You don't have to go out on a limb to say that Bill Elliott is America's most popular stock car driver. After all, he's won NASCAR's Most Popular Driver Award eight times in the last ten years.

Elliott's career really blossomed in 1985 when he shocked the motorsports world with a record qualifying lap at Daytona. Wild Bill toured the tri-oval at an average speed of 205.114 miles per hour that February. Elliott-mania was in full gear by the following week when Wild Bill won the Daytona 500.

IT HAS A RING. . .

It came as no surprise to his many loyal fans, that Bill Elliott was once again given the Winston Cup Most Popular Driver Award for 1993. McDonald's has been giving this award for ten years and eight of those awards belong to Bill. Some teams joke that the award should just be renamed "The Bill Elliott Award".

Bill gained his fame with the Melling Race Coors #9 team. He accomplished a

great deal with this team, taking 34 Winston Cup wins, 41 poles, 33 superspeedway wins and 36 superspeedway poles.

He has won the Winston Million (Daytona 500, Winston 500 and Southern 500) and once set a qualifying record at Talladega Superspeedway

LISA M. COFFMAN

Bill also set the speed record at Talladega in 1985, in this case in May, with a 209.938 mph lap.

LISA M. COFFMAN

Bill's first race car was a 1962 Ford Fairlane his dad bought for him for $50.

LISA M. COFFMAN

The Budweiser Thunderbird stops for fuel and rubber.

58

Elliott runs side by side with Ernie Irvan.

(212.809 mph). He was named the National Motorsports Press Association's Driver of the Year in 1985 and won the most-popular title six times with that team.

DAWSONVILLE = ELLIOTT

Bill's hometown (Dawsonville, Georgia) is where they built and tested the famous #9 Ford Thunderbirds. Bill was a hands-on driver, actively helping in the building and set-up of the cars. Mention Dawsonville, Georgia in the South and any stock-car fan will instantly respond, "Hey, isn't that where Bill Elliott comes from?"

THE MOVE TO JUNIOR

It was also a family team, Ernie built the engines and Dan fabricated the cars. That was great in the beginning, but as Bill got more popular the demands on his time became greater. The sponsors needed him to represent them, NASCAR needed him and of course his family wanted to see him. Finally in 1992, Junior Johnson approached Bill about driving the #11 Ford Thunderbird for him. Together with Budweiser, Junior and Bill decided to go after the championship again.

"Junior approached me a number of years ago to come drive for him, but the circumstances

Elliott sticks his nose in front of Chad Little.

As a boy growing up, Bill wasn't sure he wanted to be a race car driver. It was his father who saw his potential behind the wheel.

LISA M. COFFMAN

Elliott gets some advice between practice runs.

LISA M. COFFMAN

Elliott thrives on running in traffic!

never did work out. This time things worked out, and with Anheuser-Busch involved, I just felt like it was a perfect match. So I said, 'Hey, let's do it and go for it,' " said Elliott. Bill's first year with the new team had lots of ups and downs. There was a lot of bugs to work out. 1993 was a good year for this team. Everyone has gotten used to each other. The team was working together and Bill was in the top ten again.

BACK TO THE ROOTS

Bill had also put together his own Busch Grand National team that sported the Budweiser spon-

sorship and the #11 number. He was running the usual limited schedule that a lot of other Winston Cup drivers run: when the Busch Grand National races on the same weekend as the Winston Cup, he races in both.

This team also goes back to Bill's roots. He's building and maintaining these cars at the Dawsonville location. Bill's nephew, Casey Elliott, is also using these premises for his Busch Grand National and All Pro cars.

Casey's dad Ernie is still with the Melling Racing team as engine builder. He has also built engines for Brett Bodine's #26 Quaker State Thunderbird team.

For all the glory and recognition, Elliott is still pretty much the same regular guy he was a decade ago.

Wild Bill was the Winston Cup champion in 1988.

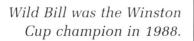

MARK MARTIN

KING OF THE SHORT TRACKS

Driving the Winston Cup #6 Roush Racing/Valvoline, and the Busch Grand National #60 Winn-Dixie Ford Thunderbirds is Mark Martin. Mark decided long ago that just racing isn't his idea of fun—he races to win.

No one could touch him last year on the Winston Cup short tracks. The most amazing story in 1993 was his Busch Grand National performances.

Whenever the Winston Cup and Busch Grand National series were scheduled on the same weekend, Mark raced in both races. If he finished the

Mark Martin drives the #6 Valvoline Ford in Winston Cup competition.

The 1993 season found Martin to be the King of the Short Tracks.

BARRY C. ALTMARK

Martin's crew flies into action during a pit stop.

Martin, a little battered but still moving, leads Kyle Petty down the front stretch.

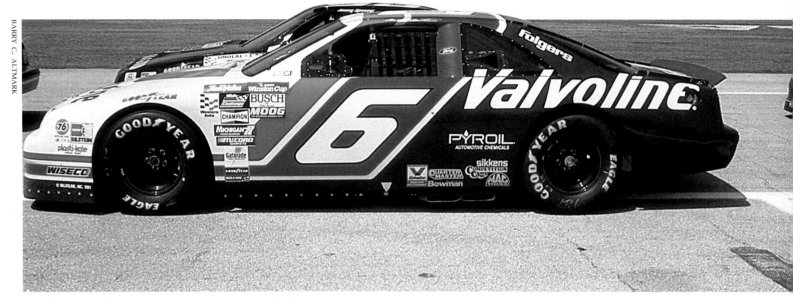

Mark was a four-time ASA champion before moving to Winston Cup action.

*Mark is known as a
team player and a
clean racer.*

*In 1993, in Busch Grand National action,
Mark won every race he finished. His
day either ended early or he won—nothing in between.*

65

Mark knows how physically demanding this sport can be. He is a dedicated bodybuilder.

Mark came within 86 points of winning the Winston Cup championship in 1990.

Because of Martin's innovations, many teams now have weight rooms and fitness programs.

Here's how Mark Martin looked before the start of the 1994 Daytona 500.

Martin doesn't race for fun—he races to win!

Martin shares a moment before a Busch Grand National race with Ward Burton.

Busch Grand National race, he won it! That's right, he won each Busch Grand National event that he finished in 1993.

The Busch Grand National regulars must have been pretty perplexed at Mark's record. He either crashed, blew an engine or won. Nothing in between.

Mark was a four-time ASA champion (1978, 1979, 1980 and 1986) before coming into the Winston Cup series. He almost became Winston Cup champion in 1990, but Dale Earnhardt decided to hold on to win. Mark lost by only 86 points. Mark's driving was so aggressive in the championship battle that a rumor was going around in the pits that Earnhardt was having problems concentrating because he kept asking about Mark's position.

The architect of Mark's Winston Cup team is Steve Hmiel who started out as his team manager then took over the crew chief duties after Robin Pemberton left for Kyle Petty in 1992.

Mark is known as a team player and a clean racer. When the Roush Endurance Race team needed some help with the driving chores at Daytona, Mark volunteered to help out. He was also the first Winston Cup driver to realize how physically demanding the series can be. He started a physical fitness program and became a dedicated body builder. He soon discovered that the better condition he's in, the more stamina he has, and the easier it is to win races. Soon other drivers took notice and most major teams now have weight rooms and fitness programs—not only for their drivers but for the entire crew.

PART IV

ON THE TRACK

SPEEDWEEK 1994

MARLIN GIVES STERLING PERFORMANCE

WINS DAYTONA 500;
JINX ON EARNHARDT REMAINS UNBROKEN

For the first time, a rookie sat on the pole as the cars lined up on the starting grid for the 36th annual Daytona 500. Loy Allen Jr. from Raleigh, North Carolina was up front, having qualified in his Ford Thunderbird at 190.158 miles per hour. Of course, only 16 of the last 35 pole winners had even finished the 500. The pack consisted of 25 Fords, 12 Chevys and five Pontiacs.

It was hot on the track. A thermometer in Allen's car before the start read 101 degrees, and the car was not going to cool off once the engines fired up! One-hundred and sixty thousand fans were in the stands. The purse was $2.8 million!

One of the safety improvements on the 1994 cars are flaps on the roof that flip upward when the car makes contact with something or gets backwards on the track. In theory, these flaps will catch the wind and hold the car down, to prevent problems with cars going airborne and flipping over after spinning out.

COWBOY DROPS THE GREEN

Troy Aikman, quarterback on the Super Bowl-champion Dallas Cowboys, dropped the green flag. Ernie Irvan led the first lap, moving out front from

A beautiful view of the start of the 1993 Daytona 500 with Kyle Petty sitting on the pole.

PAUL W. COCKERHAM

69

A crash on Lap 79 ended Todd Bodine's day during the 1994 race.

An innovation in 1994 are the roof flaps on all cars that pop up if the car hits something hard, as Harry Gant's car just has. The flaps help keep the car from going airborne and flipping over.

JANINE PESTEL

BARRY C. ALTMARK

BARRY C. ALTMARK

his starting position in the second row. Earnhardt soon passed Irvan on the inside, taking Jeff Gordon with him.

Last year's 500-winner, Dale Jarrett, had a long row to hoe ahead of him if he wanted a repeat victory. Because of a problem in the qualifying race, Jarrett had to accept a provisional spot in the starting field. He began the race in 41st position.

John Andretti, a convert from Indy cars, broke a rocker arm in the valve train in the first ten laps and spent a long time sitting in the pits. By the time he got back on the track he was 14 laps down, the only car in the race at that point that was not on the lead lap.

Irvan took the lead back at lap 15 and Irvan and Earnhardt pulled away from the rest of the pack. Jeff Gordon, riding in third, radioed his pit crew to say that everyone was getting loose in turn three.

By this time pole-sitter Loy Allen had dropped to 19th position.

FIRST YELLOW

The first caution flag of the day came out at the 20th lap with metal debris on the back stretch from Bobby Labonte's car. This gave everyone—and we mean everyone—an opportunity to come into the pits, get fresh rubber, and adjust their setups which had been designed during Speedweek under much cooler track temperatures.

The metal that came off Labonte's car did not

affect the car's performance, however, and he continued to run well.

When the cars emerged from pit row, Jeff Gordon—who won the Busch Clash the previous weekend and became engaged to be married during this year's Speedweek—was the new leader. The second the green flag returned on lap 26, Earnhardt moved into the lead drawing Lake Speed with him in the draft into second place. Gordon found himself out of the draft line and dropped all the way into 11th place.

MAJOR CRASH

The first major incident of the day took place in turn four on lap 63. Kyle Petty, Jeff Burton, John Andretti, Harry Gant, Robert Pressley, Rusty Wallace, Hut Stricklin, Chuck Bown, Sterling Marlin

and Bobby Hillin were all involved.

The accident started when Robert Pressley hit the outside wall. Chuck Bown tried to avoid hitting him and instead hit Kyle Petty, starting the chain reaction. The scattering of damaged vehicles closed pit row for several laps. Bill Elliott was in the middle of the action, but, amazingly, managed to thread his way though the chaos and was untouched.

Top right: Ward Burton and his #31 Hardee's team moved up to Winston Cup from Busch Grand National for the 1994 season.

Below: Up and coming rookie Hermie Sadler is a new star of the Busch Grand National circuit. He finished 12th at the Goody's 300 at Daytona, held the day before the Daytona 500.

Bottom right: Ricky Craven had hoped to do well at the Goody's 300, but engine failure caused him to finish 35th.

BARRY C. ALTMARK

The pace car leads the pack around the Daytona track before the start of the Goody's 300.

Dale Earnhardt has never won the Daytona 500—but in all other races held at Daytona he dominates. Here he leads the Goody's 300 on his way toward his fifth consecutive victory in the race.

Many of the cars, though badly beaten up, had the sheet metal yanked off their tires and got back on the track, hoping to gather a few more points toward the Winston Cup championship before they called it a day.

One of these drivers was Harry Gant, who was driving in his final Daytona 500. Gant managed to get around the track a couple of times with a badly damaged car before he pulled it behind the wall.

After the long yellow, Todd Bodine—who started in the 11th position—moved to the lead, with Gordon second and Earnhardt third. That was the way it was when the green flag returned at lap 70.

PROBLEM IN TURN THREE

Another major incident quickly followed in turn three. Both Brett and Todd Bodine, Ted Musgrave, Michael Waltrip and Jimmy Spencer were taken out of the race by the crash, although no one was injured.

The crash occurred when Jeff Gordon tapped Todd Bodine in the rear, sending an oil-spewing Bodine spinning wildly. Others crashed trying to avoid the accident, and some were sent sideways when they hit Todd Bodine's oil.

Dale Earnhardt cracked his windshield in the accident, and though here were two spare windshields in Earnhardt's pits, but it was not replaced as the crack was in a place where it did not obstruct Earnhardt's vision.

Jeff Gordon, who got the accident started, ended up leading the race. When the green flag fell again, Chad Little moved into the lead. Little quickly gave way to Mark Martin, who paced the pack for a time.

MIDWAY

Almost to the halfway point in the race, Earnhardt was back in the lead, leading a seven-car pack through the 31-degree banked turns. Morgan Shepherd took the lead and became the first car of the day to try to pull away from the drafting chain. But Shepherd couldn't sustain it and soon it was Mark Martin's turn again to be the first car across the start-finish line. It may have only been lap 100, but it seemed more like lap 200 the way the drivers were fighting for the lead.

Amazingly, at the 300-mile point there still had not been a car leave the race with engine failure. This fact was particularly astounding because of the heat.

It took Sterling Marlin a long time to score his first Winston Cup victory, but when it finally happened it was a big one. Marlin took the checkers at the 1994 Daytona 500.

In the International Race of Champions at Daytona, Dale Earnhardt (green) and Mark Martin (purple) get a little too close.

Mark Martin (#60) tries to hold off the charging Sterling Marlin (#4) and Michael Waltrip (#30) in the Goody's 300.

*At Daytona
some fans have
so much fun
that they don't
even see the race.*

PAUL W. COCKERHAM

ELLIOTT PLAYS HIS CARDS RIGHT

The fourth yellow flag of the race occurred at the 140-lap point, right after most of the cars had been forced to pit for the first time under the green.

The yellow, which came out when debris was discovered in the second turn, was particularly advantageous for Bill Elliott, who was one of the few who did not pit under the green.

At that point Elliott had gone a once-impossible 61 laps without refueling. When Elliott left the pits there were only 59 laps remaining in the race, so this was Elliott's final pit stop of the day.

Getting fuel and fresh rubber while the caution flag was out enabled Elliott to get back onto the lead lap.

After 355 miles there had been 12 leaders, 30 lead changes, and the average speed was 155.696.

41ST TO FIRST

Defending Daytona 500 champion Dale Jarrett had difficulties on the restart and had to slow down. Jarrett headed straight for the pits where it was decided to call it a day.

It had been a wild ride for Jarrett. He had gone from 41st to first before a burnt piston took him off the leader pace. Jarrett was only the eighth driver to drop out of the race.

The record for most different drivers to lead a

Daytona 500 was 15. With 100 miles left to go in this race, 13 different drivers had crossed the start-finish line in the lead. Ernie Irvan had led the most at this point, leading for 69 of the 160 laps that had been completed. Irvan did not look at this point as if he wanted to give up the lead again.

LAST 10%

With 50 miles left the average speed for the race 153.977. Dale Earnhardt's chances for winning his first Daytona 500 took a blow at this point when he developed difficulty with his car's handling.

All of a sudden, Earnhardt was pushed up high on a turn and started to battle his steering wheel as if he were driving on a quarter-mile dirt track. Around the same time Ernie Irvan had a problem and dropped back suddenly.

Sterling Marlin moved into the lead. Terry Labonte, driving in his 16th Daytona 500, was right on Marlin's tail and Jeff Gordon was in third. Mark Martin ran fourth. Irvan regained full running strength after dropping back to fifth place.

With four laps left to go, four drivers pulled away from the rest of the pack, Marlin, Irvan, Gordon and Terry Labonte. Marlin continued to lead and Irvan set himself off right on Marlin's bumper to attempt a last second shotgun into the lead. But Irvan couldn't pull it off and Sterling Marlin, in his 279th attempt, won his first Winston Cup race in the biggest one of all, the Daytona 500.

The 36-year-old Marlin, who is the son of former racing star Coo Coo Marlin, said after the race, "It gives me a lot of satisfaction to win a race. I knew I could do it if I got with the right race team."

There are fans, and then there are fans!

PAUL W. COCKERHAM

EARNHARDT WINS AT TALLADEGA!

GIVES HIMSELF BELATED BIRTHDAY PRESENT!
by Michael Benson

JANINE PESTEL

The Winston Select 500 was run at the 2.66-mile Talladega Superspeedway in Talladega, Alabama, on May 1, 1994. The temperature at the dropping of the green flag was a perfect 72 degrees.

Before the race started, an ever-diminishing threat of rain took some of the shine off of the afternoon—as had the death, earlier that day, of three-time Formula One champion Ayrton Senna, who had been killed in a wreck during the Grand Prix of San Marino.

At Talladega, the race started under cloudy skies, but the sun soon came out and the great majority of the laps were run under sunny conditions.

Sitting on the pole for the race was Ernie Irvan with a qualifying speed of 193.298 mph. Sitting beside him on the starting grid was rookie and Daytona-polesitter Loy Allen. Irvan took the #28 Havoline Ford to the lead immediately and led a tightly-knit pack of 42 cars through the initial laps.

Jeff Gordon, the young buck who defines the word potential around NASCAR these days, made an impressive move at the start of the race. Gordon started the race in 40th position, but was claiming the 20th spot by lap 10.

Irvan subsequently reported looseness in his rear end and dropped back to third place, allowing "The Intimidator" Dale Earnhardt to move into the lead.

IDIOTS IN THE CROWD

The first yellow flag of the day came with 170 laps remaining when Geoff Bodine smacked the wall hard in turn three and drove his disabled vehicle immediately behind the wall. This gave Irvan a chance to have his spoiler adjusted.

Dale Earnhardt celebrates in Victory Lane after winning the 1994 Winston Select 500 at Talladega.

75

JANINE PESTEL

Ernie Irvan (#28) and Dale Earnhardt (#3) battle it out for the lead while Jimmy Spencer (#27) approaches quickly from the rear. According to some drivers, Spencer's aggressiveness had been the cause of several accidents in recent weeks.

JOSEPH PESTEL

The first big wreck of the day took place on the front stretch, near the start-finish line. The accident started when Greg Sacks made contact with Todd Bodine.

As the cars hit the pits, the frontrunners were complaining, believe it or not, that cans were being thrown out of the grandstand. At least some of the cars had been struck by the projectiles. The perpetrators should have been arrested for attempted murder.

Bodine, who was not injured in his incident, said that he couldn't be sure that his accident was caused by something thrown from the crowd, but he did state that he thought he had hit something on the track.

When the green flag came back, Earnhardt retained his lead. Closely in pursuit was Todd Bodine. But Irvan's car was back to snuff and gaining

JOSEPH PESTEL

Todd Bodine's car careened into the infield. After a long time in the pits, Todd was able to return to the race and was running at the finish in 25th place.

JANINE PESTEL

The US Air team has a little trouble with this pit stop, with gasoline splashing everywhere.

JANINE PESTEL

Three abreast at Talladega! From top to bottom: Bill Elliott, Jeff Gordon and Jeff Purvis.

JANNE PESTEL

quickly. By lap 30, it was the man from Modesto, California who was back in the lead.

NEW FACES UP FRONT

Some faces at the front of the pack hadn't been seen among the leaders in any race for a while. Greg Sacks was running extraordinarily well. By lap 40, Wally Dallenbach Jr., driving for Richard Petty's STP team, had pushed his way up to fifth place. He had failed to qualify the car on the first day and had started the race in 35th position.

Dick Trickle, days before the race, had borrowed an engine from the Dale Earnhardt team. Trickle was making that engine work for him and was running in fourth place, only two positions behind Earnhardt himself.

With one quarter of the race gone, Dale Earnhardt once again took the lead, then lost it almost imme-

diately to Sterling Marlin. Jeff Gordon pushed into second place. Then both were passed by an insistant Earnhardt.

The average speed for the race with 50 laps in the books was 173.921. All but one car was still on the lead lap, that being Geoff Bodine, whose car was still being worked on in the garage area after his crash. In the meantime, on lap 55, brother Todd Bodine pushed into the lead. Todd, however, was put a lap down subsequently because of a stop and go penalty he received for leaving the pits too fast.

PITTING UNDER THE GREEN

Because there had been only one yellow flag, the pack was forced to pit for the first time under the green with 120 laps remaining. Drafting is so important at Talladega. Cars even like to pit with a

dancing partner (or two or three) so that they can immediately be involved with a draft upon leaving pit road.

Coming out of the mayhem of servicing, Michael Walrip was in the lead. Once everyone had pitted and the cars had returned to speed however, it was Ernie Irvan in first place, Earnhardt in second and Greg Sacks in third.

With less than 100 laps left to run, Irvan had led well more than half of the race, yet he had been unable to distance himself from a sizeable front pack that rarely shrank to less than six cars.

MARTIN'S WILD RIDE

Soon thereafter, there was a tremendous crash when Greg Sacks made contact with Todd Bodine near the start finish line. Bodine hit Jeff Gordon. This started a chain reaction that sent Mark Martin on a tremendous adventure through two retaining walls and into a third without any brakes. Jeff Burton and Loy Allen were also involved.

The whole crowd breathed a sigh of relief when Martin climbed out of his #6 Valvoline Ford—a little shook up but with everything in operating

The second big crash took place only ten laps after the first, and also on the front stretch—this time heading into turn one. Wally Dallenbach (#43) in Richard Petty's STP car was through for the day.

JOSEPH PESTEL

JOSEPH PESTEL

Rusty Wallace was not able to continue after the Lap 112 incident.

79

Terry Labonte's car looks like it's going to need a bit of body work!

Ernie Irvan leads the inside draft through one of Talladega's steeply banked turns.

JANINE PESTEL

order. No drivers were seriously injured in the incident.

The national televison audience watching on the ESPN Cable Network got an incredible view of the crash from Martin's front-mounted camera. The camera functioned beautifully throughout— and was still operating even after Martin's car had come to a rest.

"It scared me a little bit there. I thought that might be a bad one. Thank goodness for those roof flaps, we didn't get sideways or upside down. Thank goodness for NASCAR rules . . . I'm okay. It hurt bad, though," Martin said only a few minutes after the crash.

ENCORE

The track was picked up and racing returned—but not for long. Only a few laps after the green flag once again flew there was another crash in almost the same spot, this one bigger than the first, with close to a quarter of the pack taken out of the race.

Jimmy Spencer tapped the rear end of Terry Labonte hard enough to turn him sideways in heavy traffic. Labonte drifted into the outside wall and then careened back into traffic. To avoid hitting him several cars spun and went nose first into the outside wall, including Rusty Wallace. When all cars came to a stop, the pavement was covered

TALLADEGA FACTS

Location:	Talladega, Al
Bank In The Corners:	33 Degrees
Bank In The Tri-Oval:	18 Degrees
Bank On The Straightaways:	0 Degrees
Opened:	1969
Qualifying Record:	212.809 mph (Bill Elliott, April 30, 1987)
500-Mile Speed Record:	186.288 mph (Bill Elliott, May 5, 1985)

with skid marks all the way from the end of the front stretch through turn one. Amazingly, all drivers were okay.

"It was totally unnecessary. There are guys who are driving like it is the last lap, in the middle, trying to bully their way through. So we get 10-car accidents," said Rusty Wallace, minutes after the crash.

Wallace had suffered a tremendous crash at the 1993 Winston at Talladega—breaking ribs as he tumbled down the front stretch, literally flying over the start-finish line—so Rusty had no doubt been hoping that he would make it through this year's race without making contact with anything but air.

CRITICAL OF "IMPATIENCE"

Many drivers, including Ward Burton, were critical of the "impatience" that had seen out on the track. "I had a car that was capable of running up front, and I was looking forward to showing that," Burton said.

This time, when the wreckage was cleared, Dale Earnhardt was in the lead. The two back-to-back crashes, and long yellow flag periods, dropped the average speed for the race to under 155 mph.

With 65 laps to go, Irvan returned to the lead, drawing Jimmy Spencer with him, pushing Earnhardt back into third. Ken Schrader, in the Kodiak Chevrolet, was running in fourth place with one-third of the race remaining.

With 50 laps left in the race, Irvan got real loose and almost hit the wall. He had dropped back to tenth place before he was able to get the car back up to speed. This allowed Earnhardt to return to the lead.

BATTLE TO THE FINISH

With 34 laps remaining, Jimmy Spencer moved into the lead for the first time on the day and on the season. He showed a fleeting ability to put distance between himself and the pack as he led for a whole lap and then pulled his car into the pits for his final pit stop of the day. He was followed by seven of the other cars in the top ten.

Before everyone got a chance to pit under the

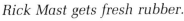

Rick Mast gets fresh rubber.

JANINE PESTEL

green, Kirk Shelmerdine made contact with the wall, bringing out the fourth yellow flag of the day, but was still able to drive his car into his pit for repairs.

During the yellow, Sterling Marlin was the leader in the #4 Kodak Film Chevrolet. Marlin held the lead for several laps after the green flag returned, but was then passed by Jimmy Spencer and Lake Speed, who went by on the inside sharing a two-car draft.

Spencer, Marlin, Earnhardt and Irvan battled at the front with ten laps left to go. Michael Waltrip pushed his nose into the picture with three laps to go. Earnhardt was still in front, M. Waltrip second, Ken Schrader moved into third and Irvan into fourth.

On the last lap it was Earnhardt and Irvan in a dogfight to the finish, with Earnhardt winning by less than a car-length. It was his 63rd career Winston Cup victory. For Earnhardt, who turned 43 the previous Friday, this win at Talladega was a belated birthday present.

WINSTON SELECT 500 RESULTS-TALLADEGA SUPERSPEEDWAY

Talladega, AL-2.66 Mile Banked Paved Speedway

May 1, 1994-Purse: $1,065,261

Fin Pos	Str Pos	Car No	Driver	Team	Laps	Total Money Won	Reason Out Of Race
1	4	3	Dale Earnhardt	Chevrolet	188	$94,865	Running
2	1	28	Ernie Irvan	Ford	188	67,990	Running
3	8	30	Michael Waltrip	Pontiac	188	50,995	Running
4	5	27	Jimmy Spencer	Ford	188	32,570	Running
5	7	25	Ken Schrader	Chevrolet	188	33,540	Running
6	6	77	Greg Sacks	Ford	188	19,905	Running
7	18	15	Lake Speed	Ford	188	28,300	Running
8	10	4	Sterling Marlin	Chevrolet	188	26,850	Running
9	12	21	Morgan Shepherd	Ford	188	25,550	Running
10	11	29	Steve Grissom	Chevrolet	188	18,600	Running
11	17	16	Ted Musgrave	Ford	188	20,495	Running
12	39	40	Bobby Hamilton	Pontiac	188	21,915	Running
13	27	42	Kyle Petty	Pontiac	188	23,185	Running
14	16	17	Darrell Waltrip	Chevrolet	188	19,005	Running
15	19	90	Mike Wallace	Ford	188	15,325	Running
16	22	71	Dave Marcis	Chevrolet	188	14,235	Running
17	28	26	Brett Bodine	Ford	188	17,420	Running
18	26	23	Hut Stricklin	Ford	187	10,180	Running
19	30	11	Bill Elliott	Ford	187	16,790	Running
20	25	1	Rick Mast	Ford	187	17,130	Running
21	9	18	Dale Jarrett	Chevrolet	186	20,860	Running
22	41	22	Bobby Labonte	Pontiac	186	15,940	Running
23	13	33	Harry Gant	Chevrolet	184	15,730	Running
24	40	24	Jeff Gordon	Chevrolet	184	15,525	Running
25	33	10	Ricky Rudd	Ford	180	9,045	Running
26	42	52	Kirk Shelmerdine	Ford	179	11,265	Running
27	14	12	Chuck Bown	Ford	168	15,110	Running
28	3	75	Todd Bodine	Ford	160	11,155	Running
29	36	14	John Andretti	Chevrolet	128	14,800	Engine
30	29	55	Jimmy Hensley	Ford	121	10,745	Accident
31	31	98	Derrike Cope	Ford	115	10,115	Accident
32	21	5	Terry Labonte	Chevrolet	112	19,060	Accident
33	20	2	Rusty Wallace	Ford	112	20,730	Accident
34	35	43	Wally Dallenbach	Pontiac	112	8,500	Accident
35	32	51	Jeff Purvis	Chevrolet	112	8,470	Accident
36	38	32	Dick Trickle	Chevrolet	112	8,440	Accident
37	24	95	Jeremy Mayfield	Ford	110	8,360	Accident
38	15	6	Mark Martin	Ford	103	20,106	Accident
39	34	8	Jeff Burton	Ford	102	12,250	Accident
40	2	19	Loy Allen	Ford	102	8,720	Accident
41	23	7	Geoff Bodine	Ford	76	12,220	Accident
42	37	41	Joe Nemechek	Chevrolet	75	8,720	Engine

LABONTE TAKES FIRST UNION 400!

KELLOGG'S CHEVY RUNS GRRRRREAT!

FIRST UNION 400 RESULTS—NORTH WILKESBORO SPEEDWAY

North Wilkesboro, NC—5/8 Mile Paved Speedway

April 17, 1994—Purse: $703,912

Fin Pos	Str Pos	Car No	Driver	Team	Laps	Total Money Won	Reason Out Of Race
1	10	5	Terry Labonte	Chevrolet	400	$61,640	Running
2	16	2	Rusty Wallace	Ford	400	42,215	Running
3	1	28	Ernie Irvan	Ford	400	41,565	Running
4	28	42	Kyle Petty	Pontiac	400	32,165	Running
5	19	3	Dale Earnhardt	Chevrolet	400	26,740	Running
6	25	10	Ricky Rudd	Ford	400	8,390	Running
7	5	7	Geoff Bodine	Ford	399	16,565	Running
8	30	33	Harry Gant	Chevrolet	399	16,850	Running
9	9	25	Ken Schrader	Chevrolet	398	15,025	Running
10	17	1	Rick Mast	Ford	397	16,130	Running
11	18	30	Michael Waltrip	Pontiac	397	13,525	Running
12	29	15	Lake Speed	Ford	397	15,975	Running
13	13	6	Mark Martin	Ford	397	17,650	Running
14	24	40	Bobby Hamilton	Pontiac	397	12,875	Running
15	12	24	Jeff Gordon	Chevrolet	396	13,100	Running
16	27	43	Wally Dallenbach	Pontiac	396	8,475	Running
17	7	4	Sterling Marlin	Chevrolet	396	15,425	Running
18	4	11	Bill Elliott	Ford	395	12,175	Running
19	26	75	Todd Bodine	Ford	395	8,025	Running
20	14	23	Hut Stricklin	Ford	395	5,950	Running
21	3	16	Ted Musgrave	Ford	395	11,800	Running
22	15	21	Morgan Shepherd	Ford	395	15,150	Running
23	2	26	Brett Bodine	Ford	395	11,525	Running
24	34	32	Dick Trickle	Chevrolet	394	5,000	Running
25	31	18	Dale Jarrett	Chevrolet	394	16,275	Running
26	36	22	Bobby Labonte	Pontiac	394	11,225	Running
27	22	98	Derrike Cope	Ford	393	7,050	Running
28	33	17	Darrell Waltrip	Chevrolet	390	10,985	Running
29	20	71	Dave Marcis	Chevrolet	388	6,800	Running
30	11	95	Jeremy Mayfield	Ford	388	5,325	Running
31	23	14	John Andretti	Chevrolet	386	10,750	Running
32	8	27	Jimmy Spencer	Ford	353	6,225	Running
33	35	8	Jeff Burton	Ford	352	9,700	Handling
34	6	77	Greg Sacks	Ford	352	4,225	Running
35	21	12	Chuck Bown	Ford	274	8,200	Engine
36	32	78	Jay Hedgecock	Ford	53	4,700	Rear End

Winner Terry Labonte's Kellogg's Chevrolet handled well throughout the day at the North Wilkesboro Speedway.

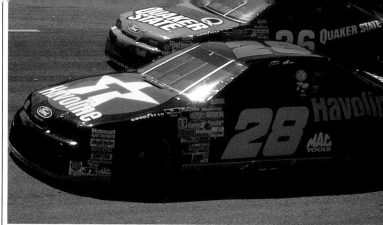

Top left: Rusty Wallace (#2) passes to the outside of Jimmy Spencer (#27) en route to a second-place finish.

Top right: Ernie Irvan (#28) and Brett Bodine (#26) are side by side through turn one.

Second from top, left: Bill Elliott prepares himself for another short-track adventure after qualifying fourth. He finished 11th.

Middle right: Dale Earnhardt (#3) closes in on Kenny Schrader (#25), looking to the low side.

Second from bottom, left: Jimmy Spencer (#27) and team-mate Bill Elliott (#11) lead Wally Dallenbach (#43) through turns 3 & 4.

Bottom right: You can see the intensity in Mark Martin's eyes.

Bottom left: Ricky Rudd's Tide Ford started the race 10th and finished sixth.

FOCUS ON PIT CREWS!

AS MANY RACES ARE WON IN THE PITS AS ON THE TRACK

by Barry Altmark

A good pit crew can fill the car with 22 gallons of fuel, clean the windshield, change four tires, make chassis adjustments and even give the driver a cold drink all in less than 20 seconds. The Winston Cup standard used to be anything under 22 seconds was great. The Rusty Wallace #2 crew changed all that in 1993 and now 18 seconds is considered a decent pit stop.

So, what happens and who is responsible for what in the pits? It may look like coordinated chaos on pit lane, but everyone out there knows exactly what his duties are and what needs to be done when. Let's take a walk around the car starting at the front:

Sign Man—Holds the pit board over the wall so the driver knows exactly where to stop. This job is very important. If the car stops too far back or too far forward it not only slows down the pit stop, but can earn the team a penalty from NASCAR. On many teams after the driver is stopped and the crew is at work, this person will take another long pole with a brush and wiper and clean the front grill and the windshield off.

Tire Man #1—Loosens lug nuts on all tires to be changed and acts as tire catcher.

Jack Man—Slides jack under car and jacks car up so tires can be changed. This position is where most teams lose their time. In one fluid motion the jack goes under the car and brings it up. If not, everyone has to wait and the entire pit stop goes into overtime.

Driver Service—It gets hot in these cars. A cold drink, maybe a towel gets passed to the driver.

Gas Man—This is the guy with the most muscles. He takes a gas tank with 11 gallons of fuel and jumps over the wall and empties his tank then goes back over the wall for another tank. That's 22 gallons of fuel. Each gas tank weighs 80 pounds when full. This is normally the only member of the pit crew to wear fire-proof clothing and a helmet. The fuel is highly flammable and could be devastating to the gas man's eyes or face.

At the start of each race, pit crews make sure their driver knows exactly where they are.

BARRY C. ALTMARK

Ernie Irvan's crew flies into action.

LISA M. COFFMAN

Mark Martin's crew provides lightning quick service.

LISA M. COFFMAN

Gas Catcher—Holds the spill-over can to catch any overflow of fuel and signals when fueling is complete. On many teams this is considered the most important job on the pit crew. When he gives the OK signal the driver hits the gas and is back in the race. A premature signal from the gas catcher and the driver can leave tires behind or leave with a gas can still attached to the car. Also, every drop of fuel is vital in Winston Cup racing. NASCAR allows only a certain amount of fuel per race. You wouldn't want to lose the race because you ran out of gas.

Tire Man #2—Pulls off loosened tires and replaces them with new tires and tightens up lug nuts. It is crucial that this tire man keep track of every lug nut. All it takes is loose or missing lug nuts and the car could very well fall out of the race with problems.

Crew Chief—The coordinator of everything. It is the crew chief's responsibility to prepare, train and coordinate everything that happens on race day on the track or in the pits. Some crew chiefs assist in the pit stop while others prefer to talk with the driver via the radio to make sure all is well. Sometimes you'll see the crew chief jump over the wall at the last second to make a chassis adjustment. The driver might complain about the car's handling or the crew chief doesn't like the way the car comes out of a corner. He must make decisions and act in mere seconds.

Miscellaneous Crew members
—In back of the wall you've probably noticed other crew members. Depending on the team there will usually be someone who is constantly watching and working a computer. They are normally calculating fuel mileage and lap times. There are back-up people who either hand tools and tires over the wall or sometimes help with the fuel cans. Many pit crews practice going

Tire Man #1 prepares to remove Bill Elliott's left front lug nut.

Geoff Bodine's crew works on the right-side rubber!

Remaining behind the wall, a crew member uses the world's longest windshield wiper to give Dale Earnhardt a better view.

over the wall and servicing the car over and over again to get it just right. Pit stops are becoming more important as technology and NASCAR rules are making the cars more even. As the Rusty Wallace crew proved in 1993, races can be won and lost in the pits as well as on the track. It is becoming more common to see drivers going back onto the track with better positions. You can lose a lap in the pits or you can gain positions. It takes the effort of everyone on the team to win.

LIFETIME LEADERS IN WINSTON CUP VICTORIES

1949–93 (AS OF MAY 15, 1994)

Driver	Victories	Driver	Victories	Driver	Victories
Richard Petty	200	Marshall Teague	7	Danny Letner	2
David Pearson	105	Bob Welborn	7	Billy Myers	2
Bobby Allison	84	Jim Reed	7	Marvin Porter	2
Darrell Waltrip*	84	Darel Dieringer	6	Johnny Beauchamp	2
Cale Yarborough	83	A.J. Foyt*	5	Tom Pistone	2
Dale Earnhardt*	62	Alan Kulwicki	5	Bobby Johns	2
Lee Petty	54	Ralph Moody	5	Emanuel Zervakis	2
Ned Jarrett	50	Dan Gurney	5	Jim Pardue	2
Junior Johnson	50	Dave Marcis*	5	Elmo Langley	2
Herb Thomas	49	Pete Hamilton	4	James Hylton*	2
Buck Baker	46	Bob Flock	4	Ray Elder	2
Tim Flock	40	Hershel McGriff*	4	Joe Lee Johnson	2
Bill Elliott*	39	Lloyd Dane	4	Tommy Thompson	2
Bobby Isaac	37	Ed Pagan	4	Dale Jarrett*	2
Rusty Wallace*	33	Eddie Gray	4	Brett Bodine*	1
Fireball Roberts	32	Glen Wood	4	Greg Sacks*	1
Rex White	26	Nelson Stacy	4	Bobby Hillin*	1
Fred Lorenzen	26	Billy Wade	4	Phil Parsons*	1
Jim Paschal	25	Morgan Shepherd*	4	Lake Speed*	1
Joe Weatherly	24	Charlie Glotzbach	4	Jody Ridley*	1
Jack Smith	21	Parnelli Jones	4	Bob Burdick	1
Benny Parsons	21	Dick Linder	3	Neil Cole	1
Fonty Flock	19	Frank Mundy	3	Marvin Burke	1
Speedy Thompson	19	Bill Blair	3	Denny Weinberg	1
Buddy Baker*	19	Gwyn Staley	3	Bill Norton	1
Neil Bonnett	19	Derrike Cope*	2	Buddy Norton	1
Davey Allison	19	Ken Schrader*	2	Buddy Shuman	1
Curtis Turner	17	Tiny Lund	2	Dick Passwater	1
Marvin Panch	17	Red Byron	2	Al Keller	1
Harry Gant*	16	Gober Sosebee	2	John Soares, Sr.	1
Geoff Bodine*	14				
Dick Hutcherson	14				
Ricky Rudd*	14				
LeeRoy Yarbrough	14				
Dick Rathman	13				
Tim Richmond	13				
Mark Martin*	12				
Ernie Irvan*	12				
Donnie Allison	10				
Terry Labonte*	10				
Paul Goldsmith	9				
Cotton Owens	9				
Kyle Petty*	7				

*indicates currently active drivers

BARRY C. ALTMARK

Davey Allison, 19 victories.

Bill Elliott, 39 victories.

Dale Earnhardt, more than 60 victories (the number seems to grow every week!)

Driver	Victories	Driver	Victories
Chuck Stevenson	1	Johnny Allen	1
Johnny Kieper	1	Larry Frank	1
Royce Hagerty	1	Johnny Rutherford	1
Art Watts	1	Wendell Scott	1
Bill Amick	1	Sam McQuagg	1
Dann Graves	1	Paul Lewis	1
Frankie Schneider	1	Earl Balmer	1
Shorty Rollins	1	Jim Hurtubise	1
Jim Cook	1	Mario Andretti	1
Jim Roper	1	Richard Brickhouse	1
June Cleveland	1	Mark Donohue	1
Jack White	1	Dick Brooks	1
Harold Kite	1	Earl Ross	1
Bill Rexford	1	Lou Figaro	1
Johnny Mantz	1	Jim Florian	1
Leon Sales	1	Lennie Pond	1
Lloyd Moore	1	Ron Bouchard	1
Joe Eubanks	1	Sterling Marlin*	1
John Rostek	1		

*indicates currently active drivers

Mark Martin,
12 victories.

Rusty Wallace,
31 victories.

1993 NASCAR WINSTON CUP SERIES FINAL STANDINGS

Pos	Driver Name	Points	Starts	Wins	Top 5	Top 10	Money Won
1	Dale Earnhardt	4526	30	6	17	21	$ 3,353,789
2	Rusty Wallace	4446	30	10	19	21	1,702,154
3	Mark Martin	4150	30	5	12	19	1,657,662
4	Dale Jarrett	4000	30	1	13	18	1,242,394
5	Kyle Petty	3860	30	1	9	15	914,662
6	Ernie Irvan	3834	30	3	12	14	1,400,468
7	Morgan Shepherd	3807	30	1	3	15	782,523
8	Bill Elliott	3774	30	0	6	15	955,859
9	Ken Schrader	3715	30	0	9	15	952,748
10	Ricky Rudd	3644	30	1	9	14	752,562
11	Harry Gant	3524	30	0	4	12	772,832
12	Jimmy Spencer	3496	30	0	5	10	686,026
13	Darrell Waltrip	3479	30	0	4	10	746,646
14	Jeff Gordon	3447	30	0	7	11	765,168
15	Sterling Marlin	3355	30	0	1	8	628,835
16	Geoff Bodine	3338	30	1	2	9	783,762
17	Michael Waltrip	3291	30	0	0	5	529,923
18	Terry Labonte	3280	30	0	0	10	531,717
19	Bobby Labonte	3221	30	0	0	6	395,660
20	Brett Bodine	3183	29	0	3	9	582,014
21	Rick Mast	3001	30	0	1	5	568,095
22	Wally Dallenbach Jr.	2978	30	0	1	4	474,340
23	Kenny Wallace	2893	30	0	0	3	330,325
24	Hut Stricklin	2866	30	0	1	2	494,600
25	Ted Musgrave	2853	29	0	2	5	458,615
26	Derrike Cope	2787	30	0	0	1	402,515
27	Bobby Hillin Jr.	2717	30	0	0	0	263,540
28	Rick Wilson	2647	29	0	0	1	299,725
29	Phil Parsons	2454	26	0	0	2	293,725
30	Dick Trickle	2224	26	0	1	2	244,065
31	Davey Allison	2104	16	1	6	8	513,585
32	Jimmy Hensley	2001	21	0	0	2	368,150
33	Dave Marcis	1970	23	0	0	0	202,305
34	Lake Speed	1956	21	0	0	1	319,800
35	Greg Sacks	1730	19	0	0	1	168,055
36	Jimmy Means	1471	18	0	0	0	148,205

LISA M. COFFMAN

LISA M. COFFMAN

The blue flag with the yellow stripe means:
"Move over and let the faster car past!"

Three abreast on the front stretch!

Ricky Rudd discusses his practice run with a crew member.

LISA M. COFFMAN

Pos	Driver Name	Points	Starts	Wins	Top 5	Top 10	Money Won
37	Bobby Hamilton	1348	15	0	0	1	142,740
38	Jimmy Horton	841	13	0	0	0	115,105
39	Jeff Purvis	774	8	0	0	0	106,045
40	Todd Bodine	715	10	0	0	0	63,245
41	Alan Kulwicki	625	5	0	2	3	165,470
42	PJ Jones	498	6	0	0	1	53,370
43	Joe Ruttman	417	5	0	1	1	70,700
44	Joe Nemechek	389	5	0	0	0	56,580
45	Loy Allen Jr.	362	5	0	0	0	34,695
46	Mike Wallace	343	4	0	0	0	30,125
47	Jim Sauter	295	4	0	0	0	48,860
48	Rich Bickle	292	5	0	0	0	36,095
49	Rick Carelli	258	3	0	0	0	19,650
50	John Andretti	250	4	0	0	0	24,915
51	Chad Little	216	3	0	0	0	41,140
52	Ken Bouchard	207	3	0	0	0	25,785
53	Ritchie Petty	195	3	0	0	0	22,990
54	Tom Kendall	185	2	0	0	0	32,190
55	Bob Schacht	180	3	0	0	0	20,205
56	TW Taylor	152	3	0	0	0	21,605
57	Kerry Teague	146	2	0	0	0	14,400
58	Ed Ferree	137	2	0	0	0	12,865
59	Scott Lagasse	124	1	0	0	0	7,800
60	HB Bailey	119	2	0	0	0	12,750
61	John Krebs	119	2	0	0	0	16,455
62	Dorsey Schroeder	113	2	0	0	0	13,615
63	Dirk Stephens	110	2	0	0	0	12,880
64	Jerry O'Neil	104	2	0	0	0	15,400
65	James Hylton	104	2	0	0	0	11,945
66	Mike Potter	101	2	0	0	0	11,915
67	Jerry Hill	98	2	0	0	0	12,885
68	Neil Bonnett	98	2	0	0	0	14,515
69	Ron Hornaday Jr.	97	1	0	0	0	6,660
70	Clay Young	92	2	0	0	0	14,370
71	Chuck Brown	91	1	0	0	0	6,610
72	Jay Hedgecock	85	1	0	0	0	4,780
73	Bill Sedgwick	85	1	0	0	0	8,140
74	Scott Gaylord	76	1	0	0	0	5,935
75	Steve Grissom	76	1	0	0	0	6,485
76	Jeremy Mayfield	76	1	0	0	0	4,830
77	Bill Schmitt	70	1	0	0	0	6,815
78	Butch Gilliland	67	1	0	0	0	6,765
79	Trevor Boys	63	1	0	0	0	6,510
80	Mike Skinner	58	1	0	0	0	5,180
81	John Chapman	55	1	0	0	0	6,525
82	Al Unser Jr.	55	1	0	0	0	23,005
83	Terry Fisher	52	1	0	0	0	6,040
84	Jeff Burton	52	1	0	0	0	9,550
85	Brad Teague	49	1	0	0	0	5,010
86	Richard Woodland	49	1	0	0	0	6,030
87	Norm Benning	46	1	0	0	0	5,410
88	Mike Chase	46	1	0	0	0	6,015
89	Graham Taylor	43	1	0	0	0	6,210
90	Stanley Smith	43	1	0	0	0	7,690
91	Andy Hillenburg	40	1	0	0	0	4,365
92	Wayne Jacks	40	1	0	0	0	5,980

1993 NASCAR BUSCH GRAND NATIONAL SERIES FINAL STANDINGS

Pos	Driver Name	Points	Starts	Wins	Top 5	Top 10	Money Won
1	Steve Grissom	3846	28	2	11	18	$ 336,432
2	Ricky Craven	3593	28	0	6	17	197,829
3	David Green	3584	28	0	6	16	225,747
4	Chuck Bown	3532	28	1	5	13	195,961
5	Joe Nemechek	3443	28	0	8	11	254,346
6	Ward Burton	3413	28	3	9	10	293,622
7	Bobby Dotter	3406	28	0	3	8	160,003
8	Robert Pressley	3389	28	3	8	13	254,346
9	Todd Bodine	3387	28	3	9	13	240,899
10	Hermie Sadler	3362	28	1	4	8	149,596
11	Tracy Leslie	3336	28	1	5	13	193,765
12	Mike Wallace	3213	28	0	1	9	131,473
13	Tom Peck	3211	28	0	2	9	131,622
14	Jeff Burton	3030	28	1	3	10	212,843
15	Rodney Combs	2969	27	0	0	3	111,396
16	Tommy Houston	2852	28	0	4	6	163,790
17	Joe Bessey	2834	25	0	2	5	111,168
18	Tim Fedewa	2775	25	0	1	4	91,608
19	Jack Sprague	2429	23	0	1	4	117,371
20	Terry Labonte	2399	20	0	7	10	117,371
21	Richard Lasater	2339	25	0	0	1	94,696
22	Roy Payne	2276	24	0	0	1	77,658
23	Shawna Robinson	1950	24	0	0	0	71,325
24	Mark Martin	1744	14	7	7	7	230,703
25	Larry Pearson	1662	15	0	3	6	72,568
26	Jim Bown	1564	18	0	0	1	52,483
27	Harry Gant	1526	16	0	3	4	73,513
28	Nathan Buttke	1490	17	0	0	1	41,650
29	Bill Elliott	1276	11	1	4	5	84,743
30	Michael Waltrip	1240	10	2	4	5	102,393
31	Butch Miller	1182	10	0	2	4	47,848
32	Chad Little	1171	12	0	2	3	56,508
33	Jason Keller	1137	12	0	0	1	35,558
34	Dale Jarrett	1130	10	0	2	5	65,678
35	Ken Schrader	1066	9	0	2	3	65,628
36	Randy Lajoie	1045	8	0	3	4	43,218
37	Dale Earnhardt	989	9	2	4	4	103,928
38	Dave Rezendes	949	11	0	0	1	29,163
39	Ernie Irvan	901	10	0	1	2	52,453
40	Jeff Green	894	11	0	1	1	33,150
41	Sterling Marlin	864	8	0	1	2	36,493
42	Jimmy Spencer	838	9	0	0	2	28,080
43	Phil Parsons	813	9	0	1	3	33,378
44	Rick Wilson	722	9	0	1	2	28,133
45	Ed Berrier	647	7	0	0	1	20,650
46	Troy Beebe	641	8	0	0	0	18,330
47	Bobby Hamilton	594	7	0	0	1	17,355
48	Johnny Rumley	559	5	1	1	1	21,125
49	Rick Mast	535	5	0	0	3	17,643
50	Darrell Waltrip	513	5	0	0	1	25,655

INDEX

The Busch Grand National Champion Spark Plug 300 in Charlotte, NC is underway!